Are Women Human?

Are Women Human?

Dorothy L. Sayers

Introduction by
Mary McDermott Shideler

William B. Eerdmans Publishing Company

Grand Rapids, Michigan / Cambridge, U.K.

First edition published 1971
This edition published 2005

Wm. B. Eerdmans Publishing Co.
255 Jefferson Ave. S.E., Grand Rapids, Michigan 49503 /
P.O. Box 163, Cambridge CB3 9PU U.K.
www.eerdmans.com

Printed in the United States of America

10 09 08 07 06 05   7 6 5 4 3 2 1

Library of Congress Cataloging-in-Publication Data

Sayers, Dorothy L. (Dorothy Leigh), 1893-1957.
Are women human? / Dorothy L. Sayers;
introduction by Mary McDermott Shideler.
p.   cm.
Originally published: 1971.
Contents: Are women human? — The human-not-quite-human.
ISBN 0-8028-2996-1 (pbk.: alk. paper)
1. Women — History — Modern period, 1600-   I. Title.

HQ1154.S27   2005
305.42 — dc22

2005050059

The two essays by Dorothy L. Sayers reprinted in this volume have
been taken from Miss Sayers' collection of twenty-one essays entitled
Unpopular Opinions, copyright © 1947 by Dorothy L. Sayers, and appear
by permission of the Trustees of the Estate of Miss Sayers.

Contents

Introduction

Mary McDermott Shideler

Though England, far more than America, is a man's world, Dorothy L. Sayers held her own in it, and more, as scholar, theologian, playwright, lecturer, essayist, and author of detective stories which are also admirable comedies of manners. Only three times, however — so far as I know — did she write directly on the nature and functions of women: in the two short articles here reprinted, and a section of the introduction to her translation of Dante's *Purgatory*. These are among the most penetrating analyses of women that have appeared in the twentieth century, and they are almost certainly the wittiest. Her weapon was the rapier, not the battering ram or the bomb.

But Miss Sayers was not a feminist, and she had certain doubts concerning the effectiveness of "aggressive feminism". The liberation of women was not a cause that she espoused, but a way of life that she practised on the premises that male and female are adjectives qualifying the noun "human being", and that the substantive governs the modifier. It cannot have been easy for her to follow those principles. To take only one example, she earned her degree in mediaeval literature — with first honours — in 1915 at Oxford University. As one of its earliest women students, she must often have been stung by the same lash that fifty years later was still occasionally wielded upon scholarly women there (I speak from experience). In the next to the last of her detective novels, *Gaudy Night,* Miss Sayers characterizes that attitude through one of her characters, who says, "All the men have been amazingly kind and sympathetic about the Women's Colleges [at Oxford]. . . . they are quite pleased to see us playing with our little toys."

This bitter comment refers to only one of the most widely prevalent ways in which women are relegated to a special class, and the remainder of *Gaudy Night* shows Oxford as a place where condescension toward women as such is not universal or even typical. It is, however, fairly common throughout the world, along with two other attitudes which Miss Sayers examines in connection with Dante's Beatrice: that which turns women into mother-images, inescapable sources of primitive energy but terrifying and tyrannous, and that which interprets women as somehow deviant from a male norm of humanity, and so ineffably mysterious, enticing, and perilous. Of these, Miss Sayers writes:

> . . . whereas there has been from time immemorial an Enigma of Woman, there is no corresponding Enigma of Man. . . . The sentiment, "Man's love is of man's life a thing apart; 'tis woman's whole existence" is, in fact, a piece of male wishful thinking, which can only be made to come true by depriving the life of the leisured woman of every other practical and

intellectual interest. Lovers, husbands, children, households — these are major feminine preoccupations: but not love. It is the male who looks upon amorous adventure as an end in itself, and dignifies it with a metaphysic. The great love-lyrics, the great love-tragedies, the romantic agony, the religion of beauty, the cult of the *Ewig Weibliches,* the entire mystique of sex is, in historic fact, of masculine invention. The exaltation of virginity, the worship of the dark Eros, the apotheosis of motherhood, are alike the work of man; the Fatal Woman is his discovery (and so, indeed, is the Fatal Man: Faust and Don Juan, Lovelace and Manfred are not of woman born). [Introduction to Dante's *Purgatory*]

Whether because of natural inclinations having a biological basis, or because of cultural pressures or practical necessities, women have tended to be more personal and pragmatic than men: to ask concerning their husbands and male colleagues not "What do men want?" but "What does this man want?" A *fortiori*, Freud's famous question, "What does woman want? Dear God! What does she want?" sounds to most women inexcusably frivolous or stupid.

Miss Sayers' own position on women is founded upon a strong, coherent world view in which the relations of male with female are derived from the relations of mankind — male and female — with the universe. Essential to that structure is the conviction that man is not a product of fortuitous biological developments, but that men are created to perform their special functions in the world. How and why that creation is (or was) accomplished is obscure. The situation it produces for us, however, is brilliantly clear. We are all equal in our creaturehood, whatever our sex, color, age, background, or abilities. But we are all different in the functions we were created to perform, as different as water from stones, and engineering from imaginative fiction. Therefore the primary task in living, for any human being, is to find and do the work for which he or she was created.

Are all women created to do the same work? Miss Sayers does not permit us to answer that question until we have dealt with a prior one: Are all human beings created to do the same work? Sentimentalists may hastily reply, "Yes — to serve others," or "to do good," evading the obvious with a pious cliché. The obvious answer is, "No, of course not, never in the history of man, and least of all now." It is — or should be — equally obvious that biological characteristics determine in part the kinds of work that any given human being is capable of. But degrees of bodily strength, muscular co-ordination, auditory and visual acuity, stolidity and excitability, cut across the classifications by sex, color, background, age, and intelligence.

In exploring the question of what women are physically and intellectually capable of doing, a valuable preliminary is the examination of what they have done. A recent study by Dr. Pearl Hogrefe, *Tudor Women: Commoners and Queens,* demonstrates that even in a period when women were sternly enjoined to be meek, passive, dependent creatures, in fact they were competent and respected in nearly every kind of work and stratum of society. They were businesswomen (some engaged in international trade), managers of extensive properties, full members of many craft guilds, supervisors of households on a scale comparable to a moderate-sized hotel of today, governors of counties and rulers of kingdoms. Theoretically oppressed and suppressed, actually they went firmly about the occupations which individual ability qualified them for and circumstances permitted or demanded. Some of them did their work well, and some badly; the same was true of the men. Their individual competence was correlated with their sex mainly because some kinds of training were ordinarily not available to female children. Sir Thomas More was exceptional, though not unique, in providing a classical education for his daughters, and they, though exceptionally privileged, were not unique in receiving and using their education constructively.

It is certainly easier to think in terms of men and women, black and white, wealthy and poor, educated and ignorant, than in the detailed, immediately practical terms of "this created being" and "that person with such-and-such skills and potentialities and passions". I have sometimes wondered if men could continue to indulge themselves in those generalities if women were not on hand to pick up the pieces after them — not that men alone are susceptible to this failing. Increasing numbers of women are subverting their personal (and therefore their feminine) natures by seeking earnestly to determine "my rôle as a woman" and "women's function in modern society" *before* they have examined their rôles as persons, and the function in our societies of individual persons, in contrast to classes of humanity.

Male and female are biological categories. Masculine and feminine are cultural categories. Both are impersonal classifications with real but limited usefulness. We cannot live or think effectively without classifying our experiences, but always we must ask whether the categories we are using are adequate for the problem we are considering. Thirty-odd years ago, when Miss Sayers delivered her lecture "Are Women Human?" she declared prophetically that in the modern world, only the category of personhood is adequate for meeting the needs of women, or of society as a whole. As we cannot afford to squander our natural resources of minerals, food, and beauty, so we cannot afford to discard any human resources of brains, skills, and initiative, even though it is women who possess them. Inherently, no natural or human resource is good; any can be good or evil depending upon how it is used, what work it performs. Thus,

> We should ask of an enterprise, not "will it pay?" but "is it good?"; of a man, not "what does he make?" but "what is his work worth?"; of goods, not "can we induce people to buy them?" but "are they useful things well made?"; of employment, not "how much a week?" but "will it exercise my faculties to the utmost?" And shareholders in — let us say — brewing companies, would astonish the direc-

torate by arising at shareholders' meetings and demanding to know, not merely where the profits go or what dividends are to be paid, not even merely whether the workers' wages are sufficient and the conditions of labour satisfactory, but loudly, and with a proper sense of personal responsibility: What goes into the beer? ["Why Work?"]

It may appear that the category of work, of function, is even more impersonal than the categories of sex and color. "I am a housewife. You are a teacher. She is a businesswoman." Yet where the worker is fitted by ability and training for the work, and has chosen or happily embraced it, such classifications reveal with a lovely precision how that individual human being is participating in the world, and therefore what kind of person she (or he) really is. Occupational categories are not *ipso facto* impersonal. We have made them so by not seeing to it that persons are steered into the work that is appropriate for them, and so far as possible releasing them from work for which they have no talent or liking. The stereotype, "Woman's place is in the home," was for a long time applied so indiscriminately that the inevitable reaction, while liberating many women from totally unsuitable employment in homes, has robbed many whose natural place is there of the dignity and joy they should have in doing the job that is right for them.

To be a person is to act, to work. In working we become our true selves and know ourselves and each other truly. Therefore work which is essentially trivial or shoddy, or consists of making things that are not worth making at all, diminishes the persons who engage in it at every level of production, exchange, and use. In contrast, they who love their work, and for love do it well, grow into the full measure of personhood. The gravest dangers our societies face today come as direct results of a pernicious philosophy that undervalues the work and therefore the persons who perform it. Or alternatively, it undervalues persons and therefore their work. To determine which element is prior in time or importance is less urgent than determining what we should do now, and now we can attack the problem from either direction — or better, from both at once.

The concept of work that Miss Sayers has proposed is neither puritanical nor mediaeval, but Christian. It grows from the belief that in work which is creative, human nature most nearly approaches its Creator. And for Miss Sayers, creativity is not restricted to the so-called creative arts. Building a house, typing a business letter, helping in the manufacture of well-designed and well-constructed objects for good purposes, teaching and healing and settling disputes and repairing machines are all creative functions when, through those activities, we participate in the processes which create and sustain societies and persons. Or they can be means of destruction if the result is to inhibit the healthy exchanges of life, the product is worthless or harmful, or the craftsmanship is unsound. But "to aim directly at serving the community is to falsify the work; the only way to serve the community is to forget the community and serve the work.... If your heart is not wholly in the work, the work will not be good — and work that is not good serves neither God nor the community; it only serves Mammon." ["Why Work?"] We are known by our work, as God is known by His.

The work of Miss Dorothy Sayers is all of a piece, every part supporting and supported by every other. Here I could only sketch in barest outline the manner in which her interpretation of women fits into her total conception of mankind, the world, and God. The essays here reprinted can stand alone, in the sense that one need not subscribe to her world view in order to comprehend her meaning, delight in her wit, and follow her exhortations regarding the treatment of women and being a woman. But she herself saw the problem in this larger context. Therefore her treatment of it has a balance and power which all of us, today, imperatively need.

I hope that many who read these two articles will go on from them to other of Dorothy Sayers' writings. Most closely related to the subject of women and their work are her Introduction to Dante's *Purgatory,* the essays "Why Work?" and "The Other Six Deadly Sins" in *Creed or Chaos?,* the novels *Gaudy Night* and *Busman's Honeymoon,* and her study of creative work, both human and divine, *The Mind of the Maker.*

Are Women Human?

Address given to a
Women's Society, 1938

Wthen I was asked to come and speak to you, your Secretary made the suggestion that she thought I must be interested in the feminist movement. I replied — a little irritably, I am afraid — that I was not sure I wanted to "identify myself," as the phrase goes, with feminism, and that the time for "feminism," in the old-fashioned sense of the word, had gone past. In fact, I think I went so far as to say that, under present conditions, an aggressive feminism might do more harm than good. As a result I was, perhaps not unnaturally, invited to explain myself.

I do not know that it is very easy to explain, without offence or risk of misunderstanding, exactly what I do mean, but I will try.

The question of "sex-equality" is, like all questions affecting human relationships, delicate and complicated. It cannot be settled by loud slogans or hard-and-fast assertions like "a woman is as good as a man" — or "woman's place is the home" — or "women ought not to take men's jobs." The minute one makes such assertions, one finds one has to qualify them. "A woman is as good as a man" is as meaningless as to say, "a Kaffir is as good as a Frenchman" or "a poet is as good as an engineer" or "an elephant is as good as a racehorse" — it means nothing whatever until you add: "at doing what?" In a religious sense, no doubt, the Kaffir is as valuable in the eyes of God as a Frenchman — but the average Kaffir is probably less skilled in literary criticism than the average Frenchman, and the average Frenchman less skilled than the average Kaffir in tracing the spoor of big game. There might be exceptions on either side: it is largely a matter of heredity and education. When we balance the poet against the engineer, we are faced with a fundamental difference of temperament — so that here our question is complicated by the enormous social problem whether poetry or engineering is "better" for the State, or for humanity in general. There may be people who would like a world that was all engineers or all poets — but most of us would like to have a certain number of each; though here again, we should all differ about the desirable proportion of engineering to poetry. The only proviso we should make is that people with dreaming and poetical temperaments should not entangle themselves in engines, and that mechanically-minded persons should not issue booklets of bad verse. When we come to the elephant and the racehorse, we come down to bed-rock physical differences — the elephant would make a poor showing in the Derby, and the unbeaten Eclipse himself would be speedily eclipsed by an elephant when it came to hauling logs.

That is so obvious that it hardly seems worth saying. But it is the mark of all movements, however

❦

well-intentioned, that their pioneers tend, by much lashing of themselves into excitement, to lose sight of the obvious. In reaction against the age-old slogan, "woman is the weaker vessel," or the still more offensive, "woman is a divine creature," we have, I think, allowed ourselves to drift into asserting that "a woman is as good as a man," without always pausing to think what exactly we mean by that. What, I feel, we ought to mean is something so obvious that it is apt to escape attention altogether, viz: not that every woman is, in virtue of her sex, as strong, clever, artistic, level-headed, industrious and so forth as any man that can be mentioned; but, that a woman is just as much an ordinary human being as a man, with the same individual preferences, and with just as much right to the tastes and preferences of an individual. What is repugnant to every human being is to be reckoned always as a member of a class and not as an individual person. A certain amount of classification is, of course, necessary for practical purposes: there is no harm in saying that women, as a class, have smaller bones than men, wear lighter clothing, have more hair on their heads and less on their faces, go more pertinaciously to church or the cinema, or have more patience with small and noisy babies. In the same way, we may say that stout people of both sexes are commonly better-tempered than thin ones, or that university dons of both sexes are more pedantic in their speech than agricultural labourers, or that Communists of both sexes are more ferocious than Fascists — or the other way round. What is unreasonable and irritating is to assume that *all* one's tastes and preferences have to be conditioned by the class to which one belongs. That has been the very common error into which men have frequently fallen about women — and it is the error into which feminist women are, perhaps, a little inclined to fall about themselves.

Take, for example, the very usual reproach that women nowadays always want to "copy what men do." In that reproach there is a great deal of truth and a great deal of sheer, unmitigated and indeed quite wicked nonsense. There are a number of jobs and pleasures which men have in times past cornered for themselves. At one time, for instance, men had a monopoly of classical education. When the pioneers of university training for women demanded that women should be admitted to the universities, the cry went up at once: "Why should women want to know about Aristotle?" The answer is NOT that *all* women would be the better for knowing about Aristotle — still less, as Lord Tennyson seemed to think, that they would be more companionable wives for their husbands if they did know about Aristotle — but simply: "What women want as a class is irrelevant. *I* want to know about Aristotle. It is true that most women care nothing about him, and a great many male undergraduates turn pale and faint at the thought of him — but I, eccentric individual that I am, do want to know about Aristotle, and I submit that there is nothing in my shape or bodily functions which need prevent my knowing about him."

That battle was won, and rightly won, for women. But there is a sillier side to the university education of women. I have noticed lately, and with regret, a tendency on the part of the women's colleges to "copy the men" on the side of their failings and absurdities, and this is not so good. Because the constitution of the men's colleges is autocratic, old-fashioned and in many respects inefficient, the women are rather inclined to try and cramp their own collegiate constitutions — which were mapped out on freer democratic lines — into the mediaeval mould of the men's — and that is unsound. It contributes nothing to the university and it loses what might have been a very good thing. The women students, too, have a foolish trick of imitating and outdoing the absurdities of male undergraduates. To climb in drunk after hours and get gated is silly and harmless if done out of pure high spirits; if it is done "because the men do it," it is worse than silly, because it is not spontaneous and not even amusing.

Let me give one simple illustration of the difference between the right and the wrong kind of feminism. Let us take this terrible business — so distressing to the minds of bishops — of the women who go about in trousers. We are asked: "Why do you want to go about in trousers? They are extremely unbecoming to most of you. You only do it to copy the men." To this we may very properly reply: "It is true that they are unbecoming. Even on men they are remarkably unattractive. But, as you men have discovered for yourselves, they are comfortable, they do not get in the way of one's activities like skirts and they protect the wearer from draughts about the ankles. As a human being, I like comfort and dislike draughts. If the trousers do not attract you, so much the worse; for the moment I do not want to attract you. I want to enjoy myself as a human being, and why not? As for copying you, certainly you thought of trousers first and to that extent we must copy you. But we are not such abandoned copy-cats as to attach these useful garments to our bodies with braces. There we draw the line. These machines of leather and elastic are unnecessary and unsuited to the female form. They are, moreover, hideous beyond description. And as for indecency — of which you sometimes accuse the trousers — we at least can take our coats off without becoming the half-undressed, bedroom spectacle that a man presents in his shirt and braces."

So that when we hear that women have once

more laid hands upon something which was previously a man's sole privilege, I think we have to ask ourselves: is this trousers or is it braces? Is it something useful, convenient and suitable to a human being as such? Or is it merely something unnecessary to us, ugly, and adopted merely for the sake of collaring the other fellow's property? These jobs and professions, now. It is ridiculous to take on a man's job just in order to be able to say that "a woman has done it — yah!" The only decent reason for tackling any job is that it is *your* job, and *you* want to do it.

At this point, somebody is likely to say: "Yes, that is all very well. But it *is* the woman who is always trying to ape the man. She *is* the inferior being. You don't as a rule find the men trying to take the women's jobs away from them. They don't force their way into the household and turn women out of their rightful occupations."

Of course they do not. They have done it already.

Let us accept the idea that women should stick to their own jobs — the jobs they did so well in the good old days before they started talking about votes and women's rights. Let us return to the Middle Ages and ask what we should get then in return for certain political and educational privileges which we should have to abandon.

It is a formidable list of jobs: the whole of the spinning industry, the whole of the dyeing industry, the whole of the weaving industry. The whole catering industry and — which would not please Lady Astor, perhaps — the whole of the nation's brewing and distilling. All the preserving, pickling and bottling industry, all the bacon-curing. And (since in those days a man was often absent from home for months together on war or business) a very large share in the management of landed estates. Here are the women's jobs — and what has become of them?

They are all being handled by men. It is all very well to say that woman's place is the home — but modern civilisation has taken all these pleasant and profitable activities out of the home, where the women looked after them, and handed them over to big industry, to be directed and organised by men at the head of large factories. Even the dairy-maid in her simple bonnet has gone, to be replaced by a male mechanic in charge of a mechanical milking plant.

Now, it is very likely that men in big industries do these jobs better than the women did them at home. The fact remains that the home contains much less of interesting activity than it used to contain. What is more, the home has so shrunk to the size of a small flat that — even if we restrict woman's job to the bearing and rearing of families — there is no room for her to do even that. It is useless to urge the modern woman to have twelve children, like her grandmother. Where is she to put them when she has got them? And what modern man wants to be bothered with them? It is perfectly idiotic to take away women's traditional occupations and then complain because she looks for new ones. Every woman is a human being — one cannot repeat that too often — and a human being *must* have occupation, if he or she is not to become a nuisance to the world.

I am not complaining that the brewing and baking were taken over by the men. If they can brew and bake as well as women or better, then by all means let them do it. But they cannot have it both ways. If they are going to adopt the very sound principle that the job should be done by the person who does it best, then that rule must be applied universally. If the women make better office-workers than men, they must have the office work. If any individual woman is able to make a first-class lawyer, doctor, architect or engineer, then she must be allowed to try her hand at it. Once lay down the rule that the job comes first and you throw that job open to every individual, man or woman, fat or thin, tall or short, ugly or beautiful, who is able to do that job better than the rest of the world.

Now, it is frequently asserted that, with women, the job does not come first. What (people cry) are women doing with this liberty of theirs? What woman really prefers a job to a home and family? Very few, I admit. It is unfortunate that they should so often have to make the choice. A man does not, as a rule, have to choose. He gets both. In fact, if he wants the home and family, he usually has to take the job as well, if he can get it. Nevertheless, there have been women, such as Queen Elizabeth and Florence Nightingale, who had the choice, and chose the job and made a success of it. And there have been and are many men who have sacrificed their careers for women — sometimes, like Antony or Parnell, very disastrously. When it comes to a *choice*, then every man or woman has to choose as an individual human being, and, like a human being, take the consequences.

As human beings! I am always entertained — and also irritated — by the newsmongers who inform us, with a bright air of discovery, that they have questioned a number of female workers and been told by one and all that they are "sick of the office and would love to get out of it." In the name of God, what human being is *not*, from time to time, heartily sick of the office and would *not* love to get out of it? The time of female office-workers is daily wasted in sympathising with disgruntled male colleagues who yearn to get out of the office. No human being likes work — not day in and day out. Work is notoriously a curse — and if women *liked* everlasting work they would not be human beings

⋙⋘

at all. *Being* human beings, they like work just as much and just as little as anybody else. They dislike perpetual washing and cooking just as much as perpetual typing and standing behind shop counters. Some of them prefer typing to scrubbing — but that does not mean that they are not, as human beings, entitled to damn and blast the typewriter when they feel that way. The number of men who daily damn and blast typewriters is incalculable; but that does not mean that they would be happier doing a little plain sewing. Nor would the women.

I have admitted that there are very few women who would put their job before every earthly consideration. I will go further and assert that there are very few men who would do it either. In fact, there is perhaps only one human being in a thousand who is passionately interested in his job for the job's sake. The difference is that if that one person in a thousand is a man, we say, simply, that he is passionately keen on his job; if she is a woman, we say she is a freak. It is extraordinarily entertaining to watch the historians of the past, for instance, entangling themselves in what they were pleased to call the "problem" of Queen Elizabeth. They invented the most complicated and astonishing reasons both for her success as a sovereign and for her tortuous matrimonial policy. She was the tool of Burleigh, she was the tool of Leicester, she was the fool of Essex; she was diseased, she was deformed, she was a man in disguise. She was a mystery, and must have some extraordinary solution. Only recently has it occurred to a few enlightened people that the solution might be quite simple after all. She might be one of the rare people who were born into the right job and put that job first. Whereupon a whole series of riddles cleared themselves up by magic. She was in love with Leicester — why didn't she marry him? Well, for the very same reason that numberless kings have not married their lovers — because it would have thrown a spanner into the wheels of the State machine. Why was she so bloodthirsty and unfeminine as to sign the death-warrant of Mary Queen of Scots? For much the same reasons that induced King George V to say that if the House of Lords did not pass the Parliament Bill he would create enough new peers to force it through — because she was, in the measure of her time, a constitutional sovereign, and knew that there was a point beyond which a sovereign could not defy Parliament. Being a rare human being with her eye to the job, she did what was necessary; being an ordinary human being, she hesitated a good deal before embarking on unsavoury measures — but as to feminine mystery, there is no such thing about it, and nobody, had she been a man, would have thought either her statesmanship or her humanity in any way mysterious. Remarkable they were — but she was a very remarkable person. Among her most remarkable achievements was that of showing that sovereignty was one of the jobs for which the right kind of woman was particularly well fitted.

Which brings us back to this question of what jobs, if any, are women's jobs. Few people would go so far as to say that all women are well fitted for all men's jobs. When people do say this, it is particularly exasperating. It is stupid to insist that there are as many female musicians and mathematicians as male — the facts are otherwise, and the most we can ask is that if a Dame Ethel Smyth or a Mary Somerville turns up, she shall be allowed to do her work without having aspersions cast either on her sex or her ability. What we ask is to be human individuals, however peculiar and unexpected. It is no good saying: "You are a little girl and therefore you ought to like dolls"; if the answer is, "But I don't," there is no more to be said. Few women happen to be natural born mechanics; but if there is one, it is useless to try and argue her into being something different. What we must *not* do is to argue that the occasional appearance of a female mechanical genius proves that all women would be mechanical geniuses if they were educated. They would not.

Where, I think, a great deal of confusion has arisen is in a failure to distinguish between special *knowledge* and special *ability*. There are certain questions on which what is called "the woman's point of view" is valuable, because they involve special *knowledge*. Women should be consulted about such things as housing and domestic architecture because, under present circumstances, they have still to wrestle a good deal with houses and kitchen sinks and can bring special knowledge to the problem. Similarly, some of them (though not all) know more about children than the majority of men, and their opinion, *as women*, is of value. In the same way, the opinion of colliers is of value about coal-mining, and the opinion of doctors is valuable about disease. But there are other questions — as, for example, about literature or finance — on which the "woman's point of view" has no value at all. In fact, it does not exist. No special knowledge is involved, and a woman's opinion on literature or finance is valuable only as the judgment of an individual. I am occasionally desired by congenital imbeciles and the editors of magazines to say something about the writing of detective fiction "from the woman's point of view." To such demands, one can only say, "Go away and don't be silly. You might as well ask what is the female angle on an equilateral triangle."

In the old days it used to be said that women were unsuited to sit in Parliament, because they "would not be able to think imperially." That, if it meant anything, meant that their views would be cramped and domestic — in short, "the woman's point of view." Now that they *are* in Parliament, people complain that they are a disappointment: they vote like other people with their party and have contributed nothing to speak of from "the woman's point of view" — except on a few purely domestic questions, and even then they are not all agreed. It looks as though somebody was trying to have things both ways at once. Even critics must remember that women are human beings and obliged to think and behave as such. I can imagine a "woman's point of view" about town-planning, or the education of children, or divorce, or the employment of female shop-assistants, for here they have some special knowledge. But what in thunder is the "woman's point of view" about the devaluation of the franc or the abolition of the Danzig Corridor? Even where women have special knowledge, they may disagree among themselves like other specialists. Do doctors never quarrel or scientists disagree? Are women really *not human,* that they should be expected to toddle along all in a flock like sheep? I think that people should be allowed to drink as much wine and beer as they can afford and is good for them; Lady Astor thinks nobody should be allowed to drink anything of the sort. Where is the "woman's point of view"? Or is one or the other of us unsexed? If the unsexed one is myself, then I am unsexed in very good company. But I prefer to think that women are human and differ in opinion like other human beings. This does not mean that their opinions, as individual opinions, are valueless; on the contrary, the more able they are the more violently their opinions will be likely to differ. It only means that you cannot ask for "the woman's point of view," but only for the woman's special knowledge — and this, like all special knowledge, is valuable, though it is no guarantee of agreement.

"What," men have asked distractedly from the beginning of time, "what on earth do women want?" I do not know that women, as women, want anything in particular, but as human beings they want, my good men, exactly what you want yourselves: interesting occupation, reasonable freedom for their pleasures, and a sufficient emotional outlet. What form the occupation, the pleasures and the emotion may take, depends entirely upon the individual. You know that this is so with yourselves — why will you not believe that it is so with us? The late D. H. Lawrence, who certainly cannot be accused of underrating the importance of sex and talked a good deal of nonsense upon the subject, was yet occasionally visited with shattering glimpses of the obvious. He said in one of his *Assorted Articles:*

"Man is willing to accept woman as an equal, as a man in skirts, as an angel, a devil, a baby-

face, a machine, an instrument, a bosom, a
womb, a pair of legs, a servant, an encyclopae-
dia, an ideal or an obscenity; the one thing he
won't accept her as is a human being, a real human being of the feminine sex."

"Accepted as a human being!" — yes; not as an
inferior class and not, I beg and pray all feminists, as
a superior class — not, in fact, as a class at all, except
in a useful context. We are much too much inclined
in these days to divide people into permanent categories, forgetting that a category only exists for its
special purpose and must be forgotten as soon as
that purpose is served. There is a fundamental difference between men and women, but it is not the
only fundamental difference in the world. There is a
sense in which my charwoman and I have more in
common than either of us has with, say, Mr. Bernard
Shaw; on the other hand, in a discussion about art

and literature, Mr. Shaw and I should probably find we had more fundamental interests in common than either of us had with my charwoman. I grant that, even so, he and I should disagree ferociously about the eating of meat — but that is not a difference between the sexes — on that point, the late Mr. G. K. Chesterton would have sided with me against the representative of his own sex. Then there are points on which I, and many of my own generation of both sexes, should find ourselves heartily in agreement; but on which the rising generation of young men and women would find us too incomprehensibly stupid for words. A difference of age is as fundamental as a difference of sex; and so is a difference of nationality. *All* categories, if they are insisted upon beyond the immediate purpose which they serve, breed class antagonism and disruption in the state, and that is why they are dangerous.

The other day, in the "Heart-to-Heart" column of

one of our popular newspapers, there appeared a letter from a pathetic gentleman about a little disruption threatening his married state. He wrote:

"I have been married eleven years and think a great deal of the wedding anniversary. I remind my wife a month in advance and plan to make the evening a success. But she does not share my keenness, and, if I did not remind her, would let the day go by without a thought of its significance. I thought a wedding anniversary meant a lot to a woman. Can you explain this indifference?"

Poor little married gentleman, nourished upon generalisations — and convinced that if his wife does not fit into the category of "a woman" there must be something wrong! Perhaps she resents being dumped into the same category as all the typical women of the comic stories. If so, she has my sympathy. "A" woman — not an individual person, disliking perhaps to be reminded of the remorseless flowing-by of the years and the advance of old age — but "a" woman, displaying the conventional sentimentalities attributed to her unfortunate and ridiculous sex.

A man once asked me — it is true that it was at the end of a very good dinner, and the compliment conveyed may have been due to that circumstance — how I managed in my books to write such natural conversation between men when they were by themselves. Was I, by any chance, a member of a large, mixed family with a lot of male friends? I replied that, on the contrary, I was an only child and had practically never seen or spoken to any men of my own age till I was about twenty-five. "Well," said the man, "I shouldn't have expected a woman [meaning me] to have been able to make it so convincing." I replied that I had coped with this difficult problem by making my men talk, as far as possible, like ordinary human beings. This aspect of the matter seemed to surprise the other speaker; he said no more, but took it away to chew it over. One of these days it may quite likely occur to him that women, as well as men, when left to themselves, talk very much like human beings also.

Indeed, it is my experience that both men and women are fundamentally human, and that there is very little mystery about either sex, except the exasperating mysteriousness of human beings in general. And though for certain purposes it may still be necessary, as it undoubtedly was in the immediate past, for women to band themselves together, as women, to secure recognition of their requirements as a sex, I am sure that the time has now come to insist more strongly on each woman's — and indeed each man's — requirements as an individual person. It used to be said that women had no *esprit de corps;* we have proved that we have — do not let us run into the opposite error of insisting that there is an aggressively feminist "point of view" about everything. To oppose one class perpetually to another — young against old, manual labour against brain-worker, rich against poor, woman against man — is to split the foundations of the State; and if the cleavage runs too deep, there remains no remedy but force and dictatorship. If you wish to preserve a free democracy, you must base it — not on classes and categories, for this will land you in the totalitarian State, where no one may act or think except as the member of a category. You must base it upon the individual Tom, Dick and Harry, and the individual Jack and Jill — in fact, upon you and me.

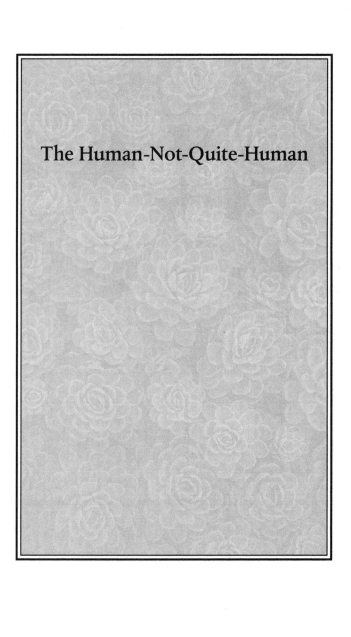

The Human-Not-Quite-Human

The first task, when undertaking the study of any phenomenon, is to observe its most obvious feature; and it is here that most students fail. It is here that most students of the "Woman Question" have failed, and the Church more lamentably than most, and with less excuse. That is why it is necessary, from time to time, to speak plainly, and perhaps even brutally, to the Church.

The first thing that strikes the careless observer is that women are unlike men. They are "the opposite sex" — (though why "opposite" I do not know; what is the "neighbouring sex"?). But the fundamental thing is that women are more like men than anything else in the world. They are human beings. *Vir* is male and *Femina* is female: but *Homo* is male and female.

This is the equality claimed and the fact that is persistently evaded and denied. No matter what arguments are used, the discussion is vitiated from the start, because Man is always dealt with as both *Homo* and *Vir,* but Woman only as *Femina.*

I have seen it solemnly stated in a newspaper that the seats on the near side of a bus are always filled before those on the off side, because, "men find them more comfortable on account of the camber of the road, and women find they get a better view of the shop windows." As though the camber of the road did not affect male and female bodies equally. Men, you observe, are given a *Homo* reason; but Women, a *Femina* reason, because they are not fully human.

Or take the sniggering dishonesty that accompanies every mention of trousers. The fact is that, for *Homo,* the garment is warm, convenient and decent. But in the West (though not in Mohammedan countries or in China) *Vir* has made the trouser his prerogative, and has invested it and the skirt with a sexual significance for physiological reasons which are a little too plain for gentility to admit. (Note: that the objection is always to the closed knicker or trouser; never to open drawers, which have a music-hall significance of a different kind.) It is this obscure male resentment against interference with function that complicates the simple *Homo* issue of whether warmth, safety, and freedom of movement are desirable qualities in a garment for any creature with two legs. Naturally, under the circumstances, the trouser is *also* taken up into the whole *Femina* business of attraction, since *Vir* demands that a woman shall be *Femina* all the time, whether she is engaged in *Homo* activities or not. If, of course, *Vir* should take a fancy to the skirt, he will appropriate it without a scruple; he will wear the houppelande or the cassock if it suits him; he will stake out his claim to the kilt in Scotland or in Greece. If he chooses (as he once chose) to deck himself like a peacock in the mating season, that is *Vir's* right; if he prefers (as he does to-day) to affront the eye with drab colour and ridiculous outline, that is *Homo's* convenience. Man dresses as he chooses, and Woman to please him; and if Woman says she ever does otherwise, he knows better, for she is not human, and may not give evidence on her own behalf.

Probably no man has ever troubled to imagine how strange his life would appear to himself if it were unrelentingly assessed in terms of his maleness; if everything he wore, said, or did had to be justified by reference to female approval; if he were compelled to regard himself, day in day out, not as a member of society, but merely *(salvâ reverentiâ)* as a virile member of society. If the centre of his dress-consciousness were the cod-piece, his education directed to making him a spirited lover and meek paterfamilias; his interests held to be natural only in so far as they were sexual. If from school and lecture-room, Press and pulpit, he heard the persistent outpouring of a shrill and scolding voice, bidding him remember his biological function. If he were vexed by continual advice how to add a rough male touch to his typing, how to be learned without losing his masculine appeal, how to combine chemical research with seduction, how to play bridge without incurring the suspicion of impotence. If, instead of allowing with a smile that "women prefer cavemen," he felt the unrelenting pressure of a whole social structure forcing him to order all his goings in conformity with that pronouncement.

He would hear (and would he like hearing?) the female counterpart of Dr. Peck[1] informing him: "I am no supporter of the Horseback Hall doctrine of 'gun-tail, plough-tail and stud' as the only spheres for masculine action; but we do need a more definite conception of the nature and scope of man's

1. Dr. Peck had disclaimed adherence to the *Kinder, Kirche, Küche* school of thought.

57

life." In any book on sociology he would find, after the main portion dealing with human needs and rights, a supplementary chapter devoted to "The Position of the Male in the Perfect State." His newspaper would assist him with a "Men's Corner," telling him how, by the expenditure of a good deal of money and a couple of hours a day, he could attract the girls and retain his wife's affection; and when he had succeeded in capturing a mate, his name would be taken from him, and society would present him with a special title to proclaim his achievement. People would write books called, "History of the Male," or "Males of the Bible," or "The Psychology of the Male," and he would be regaled daily with headlines, such as "Gentleman-Doctor's Discovery," "Male-Secretary Wins Calcutta Sweep," "Men-Artists at the Academy." If he gave an interview to a reporter, or performed any unusual exploit, he would find it recorded in such terms as these: "Professor Bract, although a distinguished botanist, is not in any way an unmanly man. He has, in fact, a wife and seven children. Tall and burly, the hands with which he handles his delicate specimens are as gnarled and powerful as those of a Canadian lumberjack, and when I swilled beer with him in his laboratory, he bawled his conclusions at me in a strong, gruff voice that implemented the promise of his swaggering moustache." Or: "There is nothing in the least feminine about the home surroundings of Mr. Focus, the famous children's photographer. His 'den' is panelled in teak and decorated with rude sculptures from Easter Island; over his austere iron bedstead hangs a fine reproduction of the Rape of the Sabines." Or: "I asked M. Sapristi, the renowned chef, whether kitchen-cult was not a rather unusual occupation for a man. 'Not a bit of it!' he replied, bluffly. 'It is the genius that counts, not the sex. As they say in *la belle Ecosse*, a man's a man for a' that' —

and his gusty, manly guffaw blew three small patty pans from the dresser."

He would be edified by solemn discussions about "Should Men Serve in Drapery Establishments?" and acrimonious ones about "Tea-Drinking Men"; by cross-shots of public affairs "from the masculine angle," and by irritable correspondence about men who expose their anatomy on beaches (so masculine of them), conceal it in dressing-gowns (too feminine of them), think about nothing but women, pretend an unnatural indifference to women, exploit their sex to get jobs, lower the tone of the office by their sexless appearance, and generally fail to please a public opinion which demands the incompatible. And at dinner-parties he would hear the wheedling, unctuous, predatory female voice demand: "And why should you trouble your handsome little head about politics?"

If, after a few centuries of this kind of treatment,

the male was a little self-conscious, a little on the defensive, and a little bewildered about what was required of him, I should not blame him. If he traded a little upon his sex, I could forgive him. If he presented the world with a major social problem, I should scarcely be surprised. It would be more surprising if he retained any rag of sanity and self-respect.

"The rights of woman," says Dr. Peck, "considered in the economic sphere, seem to involve her in competition with men in the struggle for jobs." It does seem so indeed, and this is hardly to be wondered at; for the competition began to appear when the men took over the women's jobs by transferring them from the home to the factory. The mediaeval woman had effective power and a measure of real (though not political) equality, for she had control of many industries — spinning, weaving, baking, brewing, distilling, perfumery, preserving, pickling

— in which she worked with head as well as hands, in command of her own domestic staff. But now the control and direction — all the intelligent part — of those industries have gone to the men, and the women have been left, not with their "proper" *work* but with *employment* in those occupations. And at the same time, they are exhorted to be feminine and return to the home from which all intelligent occupation has been steadily removed.

There has never been any question but that the women of the poor should toil alongside their men. No angry, and no compassionate, voice has been raised to say that women should not break their backs with harvest work, or soil their hands with blacking grates and peeling potatoes. The objection is only to work that is pleasant, exciting or profitable — the work that any human being might think it worth while to do. The boast, "My wife doesn't need to soil her hands with work," first became general when the commercial middle classes acquired the plutocratic and aristocratic notion that the keeping of an idle woman was a badge of superior social status. Man must work, and woman must exploit his labour. What else are they there for? And if the woman submits, she can be cursed for her exploitation; and if she rebels, she can be cursed for competing with the male: whatever she does will be wrong, and that is a great satisfaction.

The men who attribute all the ills of *Homo* to the industrial age, yet accept it as the norm for the relations of the sexes. But the brain, that great and sole true Androgyne, that can mate indifferently with male or female and beget offspring upon itself, the cold brain laughs at their perversions of history. The period from which we are emerging was like no other: a period when empty head and idle hands were qualities for which a man prized his woman and despised her. When, by an odd, sadistic twist of morality, sexual intercourse was deemed to be a marital right to be religiously enforced upon a meek reluctance — as though the insatiable appetite of wives were not one of the oldest jokes in the world, older than mothers-in-law, and far more venerable than kippers. When to think about sex was considered indelicate in a woman, and to think about anything else unfeminine. When to "manage" a husband by lying and the exploitation of sex was held to be honesty and virtue. When the education that Thomas More gave his daughters was denounced as a devilish indulgence, and could only be wrung from the outraged holder of the purse-strings by tears and martyrdom and desperate revolt, in the teeth of the world's mockery and the reprobation of a scandalised Church.

What is all this tenderness about women herded into factories? Is it much more than an excuse for acquiescing in the profitable herding of men? The wrong is inflicted upon *Homo*. There are temperaments suited to herding and temperaments that are not; but the dividing lines do not lie exactly along the sexual boundary. The Russians, it seems, have begun to realise this; but are revolution and blood the sole educational means for getting this plain fact into our heads? Is it only under stress of war that we are ready to admit that the person who does the job best is the person best fitted to do it? Must we always treat women like Kipling's common soldier?

It's vamp and slut and gold-digger,
and "Polly, you're a liar!"
But it's "Thank-you, Mary Atkins"
when the guns begin to fire.

We will use women's work in wartime (though we will pay less for it, and take it away from them when the war is over). But it is an unnatural busi-

ness, undertaken for no admissible feminine reason
— such as to ape the men, to sublimate a sexual re-
pression, to provide a hobby for leisure, or to make
the worker more bedworthy — but simply because,
without it all *Homo* (including *Vir*) will be in the
soup. But to find satisfaction in doing good work
and knowing that it is wanted is human nature;
therefore it cannot be feminine nature, for women
are not human. It is true that they die in bombard-
ments, much like real human beings: but that we
will forgive, since they clearly cannot enjoy it; and
we can salve our consciences by rating their bat-
tered carcases at less than a man's compensation.[2]

Women are not human. They lie when they say
they have human needs: warm and decent clothing;
comfort in the bus; interests directed immediately
to God and His universe, not intermediately

2. This last scandal did in the end outrage public opinion and
was abolished.

through any child of man. They are far above man to inspire him, far beneath him to corrupt him; they have feminine minds and feminine natures, but their mind is not one with their nature like the minds of men; they have no human mind and no human nature. "Blessed be God," says the Jew, "that hath not made me a woman."

God, of course, may have His own opinion, but the Church is reluctant to endorse it. I think I have never heard a sermon preached on the story of Martha and Mary that did not attempt, somehow, somewhere, to explain away its text. Mary's, of course, was the better part — the Lord said so, and we must not precisely contradict Him. But we will be careful not to despise Martha. No doubt, He approved of her too. We could not get on without her, and indeed (having paid lip-service to God's opinion) we must admit that we greatly prefer her. For Martha was doing a really feminine job, whereas Mary was

❦

just behaving like any other disciple, male or female; and that is a hard pill to swallow.

Perhaps it is no wonder that the women were first at the Cradle and last at the Cross. They had never known a man like this Man — there never has been such another. A prophet and teacher who never nagged at them, never flattered or coaxed or patronised; who never made arch jokes about them, never treated them either as "The women, God help us!" or "The ladies, God bless them!"; who rebuked without querulousness and praised without condescension; who took their questions and arguments seriously; who never mapped out their sphere for them, never urged them to be feminine or jeered at them for being female; who had no axe to grind and no uneasy male dignity to defend; who took them as he found them and was completely unselfconscious. There is no act, no sermon, no parable in the whole Gospel that borrows its pungency from female perversity; nobody could possibly guess from the words and deeds of Jesus that there was anything "funny" about woman's nature.

But we might easily deduce it from His contemporaries, and from His prophets before Him, and from His Church to this day. Women are not human; nobody shall persuade that they are human; let them say what they like, we will not believe it, though One rose from the dead.